My Alexandria Tales

Barbara Cousens

*Dedicated to all dogs and dog lovers everywhere
and especially to Jud, Daisy, Kiote & Lucinda.*

Contents

Boxed In

Any anxiety I might have felt at the sight of my two companions boxed into their transport crates on the day we left South Africa was marginally eradicated by the distraction of a torrential downpour at the very moment of departure.

Lightning cracked all around us with an invading precision, reminding us destiny may have had a role in the proceedings.

Some weeks prior, we had visited the pet transport company to measure up for the journey. Two of the largest crates on offer would have to be flown in all the way from Texas only to be flown out again with their precious cargo. The reaction of my golden retriever, Lucinda (often called Lucy), that day was to vomit all over the floor of the reception room while the same situation triggered in my husky Kiote (named after Don Quixote and very much a knight in most circumstances), an instant desire to devour a pet bird awaiting emigration.

First impressions were not good, and the nurse decreed the maximum dosage of "natural" tranquilizers for both of them.

Afternoon weather tensions multiplied that night as our flight was grounded indefinitely over a refueling problem. Thoughts of how my incarcerated companions would behave alongside a caged lion or even a crocodile, induced a mild degree of panic in me. I worried less about Lucy whose intellectual curiosity seldom intruded upon a more benign disposition.

It was not until we were safely winging our way northward that I could resume some composure. And so it was as I set forth on my American adventure.

DOG DAYS

Not one of us had any idea what our life would be like. We awoke to the tail end of winter and then, almost as suddenly, the burst of a northern hemisphere spring. At that point, we (all three) knew the journey had been worth it.

Old Town Alexandria heralds the spring in a particularly delectable way. Trees one never noticed suddenly burst their buds like some exotic fireworks display as they open up to a new world. Beneath them, the hyacinths and daffodils stand tall. Simultaneously, a new crop of babies turn up along with the birdsong.

Our morning walks took us uphill past multicolored town houses with adorning flower boxes and designer pots with violet and yellow pansies spilling onto the street and often, an inviting bench. If there wasn't already a "welcome" mat, the signs were obvious. There were also enough doggy smells to intrigue the canines until the play park where we turned, obediently minding the instruction to "keep off the grass," and headed east for the river. Kiote could not always wait that long and sometimes did his business along the down route, but mostly he saved it for the park, a stamp-sized patch on the river's edge. Lucy, like most females, preferred her home ground and seldom marked her spot en route.

Picking up the poop was a new exercise for me, but after a few practice runs my dexterity improved. I quickly learned to disregard the imaginings of prying onlookers and not to attempt to collect it from a thorny holly bush.

Doggone

The dogs' adaptation to their home ground was miraculous. Seriously inconvenienced by the reduced size of their new yard, Kiote nevertheless refused to be deterred from regular habits such as burying his bones, only now both ends stuck out. Lucy and I pretended not to notice.

With no other option, the master of the house generally selected the north-west corner of our tiny garden as poop corner, fastidiously piling the decorative white stones on top of his offerings. Unraveling these mini gravesites in the morning was not one of my favorite tasks, so I had to learn to tune in to the sounds of small white pebbles being overturned in the night and then, armed with a flashlight and doggy bag, I would stalk him to "scoop the poop" before he got going.

Spotting squirrels and giving chase was a favorite pastime of Lucy. She could almost climb the single tree in our yard, notwithstanding a recent operation to her cruciate ligament! In hunting mode, she would stop dead in her tracks, ears pricked and tail alerted at the horizontal. She had lost weight, and her little round tummy no longer revolved like a drum. I felt she would live long in this place.

My first excursion out of the house brought a little-anticipated result. I returned to a large warning pinned to my door from none other than the animal control officer, signed "Wylie." I didn't for a moment believe he had happened on my yodeling dogs. It was simply an unneighborly gesture that triggered the complaint. This seriously set me back as I searched for a solution. Comfort came from my Realtor who said, "Give it two months. That's all it takes."

She was right. We never heard more from the neighbor or the citation officer.

The Parks

At Windmill Park, a myriad of birds gather on the old pylons—gulls, cormorants, egrets—while Canadian geese with an occasional white duck, ripple the water below. A milky gray sky at the end of the day transforms into a deep iridescent blue at night, magically reflecting the local lamp lights. And like a Venetian seascape, the domed Capitol of Washington, D.C., diminishes in its own vanishing point.

This park is particularly romantic to me as it was here I met my partner, Jud, and his 10-year old basset, Daisy, an icon among dog owners of Old Town. At that time, she was just learning to cope with her custom-made cart to revive the use of her back legs. Undeterred by her impediment, she continued to roam the streets of Old Town, hounding out the best smells in the neighborhood. This included the local postman in the south-east quadrant whose handy treats she never forgot. Daisy eventually regained her independence using both back legs in tandem, with her tail acting as ballast —a remarkable feat for both man and dog!

Summertime sees the riverboats churning their way up and down the river, and every few seconds, the planes swoop down or ascend, signaling the buzzing world capital nearby. Here, the dogs and I often paused by the waterfront in wonder. We saw our first beaver at Windmill Park, paddling upstream a little too close for comfort, I had thought. Lucinda often swims for an hour at a time so far out that, on more than one occasion, the Coast Guard was alerted.

Jones Point is another gathering of joyful dogs of all shapes and sizes. From a blonde female bouvier— whose immaculate bouffant hair, turquoise neck tie, and pedicured feet more befit a tart at the beach— to ridgebacks and red setters in pairs, a single inimitable elk hound, and multiple labs. I have heard it said that Alexandria is the handsomest town in all Virginia, and in my opinion, Kiote and Lucinda were indeed the handsomest pair in all that City!

Medicine Man

Emigrating with two dogs grounds you in particular ways and I now fully appreciate the travails of motherhood. The worst recollection was our first weekend when Kiote, who was still registering his protest at being cooped up for so long on the international flight by refusing food, also shed a few ticks (probably carried all the way from South Africa). Convinced he at least had tick-bite fever, I phoned a vet who was on the point of closing. He told ME to take his temperature.

"With what? And how?" I thought as I rushed on instruction to the neighborhood pharmacy, only to be confronted by a shelf full of options ranging from high to low-priced, hand-held to automatic and mercury to digital thermometers. I beckoned the busy pharmacist for assistance.

Given my state of mind and consternation at the choices, she cautioned me more than once against inserting the thermometer in my own mouth after my dog's rectum. I purchased a dried pig's ear to keep him amused and prayed he would behave more in tune with his namesake than a delinquent émigré. The scene of the operation was my newly inflated bed.

After sticking the device sufficiently far up his backside for the required 60 seconds, we both became distracted by bleeping noises at 4-second intervals, which made the patient acutely aware that, despite the crackling of pork at one end, something serious was going on at the other. No one can imagine the relief I felt when I found he had a normal doggy temperature, and the instrument neither broke in situ nor was it ejected midstream.

PLAYING POSSUM

If one is going to be awakened in the middle of the night, the short discordant feminine yap elicited by Lucinda the night we (all three) discovered an opossum is a preferred option.

After being roused by her alarm, I found Kiote in the guest room standing querulously over a gibbering, pink-eyed wretch pinned to the floor in fear and very uncertain of its next move. Conforming with the gentility of his breed, Kiote too was in a somewhat statuesque trance, his eyes transfixed on the quarry, and his bushy tail coiled in heightened expectancy.

Without too much chagrin on his part, I managed to coax him back to the bedroom, barred up the door, and opened the window for the as yet unidentified alien to escape.

It wasn't until I saw the slightly blood-spattered walls the next morning I deduced there had already been a spat. Its hairy little body lay peacefully in the wicker waste basket—a last refuge for the adventurous opossum. I commended its valiant jump, notwithstanding its nocturnal injury, and was thankful, too, for the plastic lining. Gathering up its limp little body, I took it outside. Only much later, on retelling the story, was I told that the little creature could have had the edge on all of us by simply "playing possum" and escaping to more friendly climes.

Cook Out

Summertime. And a time to cook. The smell of freshly barbecued meat en route to the river induced in Kiote nostalgic memories of a traditional "braaivleis" back home. Sniffing the aroma wafting overhead, he tore off without warning or a leash in the direction of the cookout, crossing a busy street and, as luck would have it, the path of a roving Alexandria cop.

Seconds later, with sirens blazing, the city official had sped to the scene of the crime while mothers screamed and kids darted helter-skelter. My worst nightmare was materializing.

Musing on the prospect of liability and off-leash ordinances, I tore off to find a somewhat sanguine canine poised beside a rotund 300-pound pot-bellied cook turning his chops in high anticipation. Both tails were wagging. The kids were safe, and the meat was done. The cop just grinned.

I clicked into action and captured the scene on camera, diffusing the tension and inducing a few smiles. Life on the beat quickly returned to normal.

Food for Thought

We know that hunger pangs are often a craving for something far deeper than food, and so it was, some months after landing in the U.S., that I felt a twinge of desire for traditional fruitcake.

Guaranteed to stay fresh by the introduction of large dollops of brandy, its many failsafe appearances when guests turn up unexpectedly makes fruitcake, anywhere but in the U.S., the ultimate standby.

"What better to assuage the pangs of homesickness than traditional fruitcake?" I thought. My words burst out uncontrollably, "How I long for a nice piece of fruitcake!"

Silence befell the office.

"Well, what's wrong with fruitcake?" I asked.

Angela took up the challenge. A shortish woman in her fifties, she gathered up all the indignation she could muster, lifting her shoulders in the process and squaring up to look at me with fixed eyeballs. "THIS IS THE LAND OF HORRIBLE FRUITCAKE!" she declared.

A stunned silence greeted the confession.

Patty nodded in approval, remembering the many times she, herself, had re-gifted fruitcake. They expunged a great myth about American hospitality, and we all felt close that day. And I no longer felt hungry.

Incorporating Big Boxes

The great big-box cost-saving experience, endemic to the U.S. and unequaled anywhere outside it, comes at a price. Once you think on this galactic scale, it is impossible to return to earthly dimensions. Your dark side will startle you. Any prior shopping experience pales in significance.

A million bargains await to tempt every one of the would-be anonymous shoppers into a dreamlike state. While no one is looking, you can convince yourself of needs beyond your wildest dreams as you lurch up to grab at outrageously low-priced bulk buys before they either cascade down on your head or lodge themselves immovably in your overtaxed shopping cart. Toiletries and cans, juices and jams, pasta and pastries start weighing your conscience and cart alike. Every aisle engenders the Midas touch. Yet your higher self wonders: "How can it be a bargain if you don't live long enough to consume the contents?"

My overarching prayer is to preserve me from temptation and deliver me from bringing my boxed booty across the threshold of my tiny house. For as long as they last, the numerous toothbrushes in my bathroom will be a deadly reminder that sins really do come in sevens.

DEATH AND TRANSFORMATION

For a long time, we reeled after the shock of the events of 9/11. It was, of course, quite unimaginable, and one could speak volumes on the subject. Now, of course, the world is truly a different place.

On that fateful day, I was at a meeting on one of the cruise boats plying the Potomac, discussing no less than park privileges for dogs. It was so quiet and peaceful with the sun streaming in the windows as we were seated for Danish pastries and coffee. Watching some ducks float by, I remember feeling truly happy. Then at 9:15 a.m. someone got a call to say that the World Trade Center had been hit, and so it all began.

Alexandria was warned of dust fallout from the Pentagon plane crash, and, as I walked early the next morning with a few lone joggers, I witnessed a great September sunrise and blood-red river reflecting the dusty sky with starkly silhouetted wood pylons, ubiquitous ducks and some herons picking their way through the water.

Later that day, they found the last live body in the towers as families gave up hope but still paraded pictures of their missing relatives everywhere, even while the long lists of the dead were read over and over again on National Public Radio.

Thank God for faith and the ability to transcend these dastardly deeds with wonderful words, which streamed from newspapers, podiums and pulpits, and, when words failed, music and anthems. The cars, shops, buildings, and bridges bedecked with American flags and tri-colored ribbons translated into caring and politeness on the streets. Cycle rage became a thing of the past.

LEAVING AGAIN

Owning a dog brings a new attitude to going away. Precise instructions to their keeper, the local vet, would to some extent assuage my guilt at leaving, but defense of certain idiosyncracies was a more pressing need.

This is what I wrote:

"As with his illustrious namesake (Don Quixote), Kiote has been frustrated in his quest to find a windmill and/or damsel in distress in this part of the world. He could consequently show signs of an uneven temperament. If so, apply large quantities of adulation (a common curative for most males). Exerting (your) authority (over his) will not help. If you follow his rules, you will be rewarded with affection beyond measure. This can be demonstrated by a body lunge accompanied by the pinning down of one foot (yours). Providing you do not change the rules of the game, he will continue to reward you thus. Apart from copious tufts of hair on your dark apparel, there is only an upside to being the recipient of this much love. Any indication you intend immersing him in a bath, putting drops in his ears, or, worst of all, injecting him (anywhere) is likely to bring on fierce resistance usually accompanied by a high-pitched yodel. Do not be alarmed. This alpha tenor needs his voice to reassure himself and you that he is top dog."

Sugar Sweet

"Lucinda is more like sugar plum pie, but in order to induce the desired degree of sweetness, she should not be allowed to feel emotionally insecure at any time. Separation will make her nervous to a degree of hysteria (maybe even epilepsy, though this has long been in remission).

Ways to counteract the problem are incessant petting, head scratching, and tummy tickling. It is understandable that no one at your institution can be assigned to this task on a 24-hour basis. However, even occasional indications that someone, somewhere knows how to calm the patient will render her compliant and sweetness personified.

Other indications of her nervous disposition are a predisposition to eating or at least having something in her mouth at most times when she is awake. Stumpy dentures evidence past excesses in this regard. However, having lost their incisiveness, there is no fear of additional damage to her teeth, so the administration of anything chewable at any time must be regarded as low risk."

THE END

Sadly both dogs are now dead, Lucinda from a huge cantaloupe-sized tumor in her spleen and Kiote from suspected spinal cancer.

We had quality time with both of them before they drew their last breaths. Stroking and hugging each one in a vain attempt to prolong the dying moments.

The week before she died, Lucinda had walked with us at Founders Park and, despite a mouth full of sores, she still managed to strain on the leash and salivate at the sight of ducks. Such was her spirit.

As she drew her last breaths, she placed her head on her paw, just as she had done as a pup and, from a tension-filled, vexed little face, her expression became calm and youthful. But she would not look at us.

Kiote, at the end, displayed the same traits that had imbued his life. Energized by new surroundings and intrigued by the smells of a quiet hospital at 4 a.m., he bade us goodbye with a couple of well-directed licks and then looked up at the vet with raised eyebrows as if to conduct his own finale.

Both lived comparatively long lives but never long enough in human terms. They squeezed meaning into every moment, connected us with things of importance, and left us indelible memories. We are still together through the places we enjoyed, the people we met, and the dogs we knew. All enfolding us in tales of My Alexandria.

About the Author

Barbara Cousens came to the U.S. from her native South Africa in 2001. A coveted green card was the catalyst.

After running her own public relations practice in South Africa for 20 years, she settled on the East Coast electing as her companions her two dogs, Kiote and Lucinda.

Having eliminated other options such as the West Coast (too far) and New York City (too fast), she found Alexandria, Virginia, on the banks of the Potomac River just right. Its history, human scale, and dog-friendliness marked the spot. She deliberately avoided driving for 3 months in order to condition herself to "the right side" of the road and soon settled into a life of pedestrian peace.

Walking heightened her instincts, and most of her stories are based on early adventures in the first 6 months as encapsulated in Barbara's letters home to friends and family. All struck a memorable chord.

Barbara is now a Realtor in Alexandria.